RAZZMATAZZ

A FANFARE OF POETRY

RAZZMATAZZ

A Fanfare of Poetry

JENNIFER P. LUMLEY

iUniverse, Inc.
Bloomington

RAZZMATAZZ
A Fanfare of Poetry

iUniverse books may be ordered through booksellers or by contacting:

iUniverse
1663 Liberty Drive
Bloomington, IN 47403
www.iuniverse.com
1-800-Authors (1-800-288-4677)

ISBN: 978-1-4759-0264-8 (sc)
ISBN: 978-1-4759-0266-2 (e)
ISBN: 978-1-4759-0265-5 (dj)

Printed in the United States of America

iUniverse rev. date: 4/17/2012

Cover Design and Graphics by Maurice Fletcher
Photography by Maurice Fletcher and Jennifer P. Lumley
Art Work and Illustrations by Jennifer P. Lumley

Epigraph

"When all your desires are distilled
You will cast just two votes:
To love more,
And be happy."

Hafiz of Persia

* * * * * * * * * * * * * * *

"Poetry: the best words in the best order"

Samuel Taylor Coleridge

"RAZZMATAZZ"

is a rare combination of fun,
dynamic, entertaining and spontaneous
yet insightful and thoroughly
prepared book of poetry.

Preface

"RAZZMATAZZ", A Fanfare of Poetry", takes a lighter look at poetry. There is no hidden source of inspiration or secret to the popularity and success of the pieces included. Rather, the beautiful adventure and excitement for life throughout the day, early in the mornings or very late at nights, are the cornerstones upon which these fun-filled poems have been created. They have brought laughter and cheer to adults and young ones alike.

"RAZZMATAZZ" showcases the Author's versatility, as she easily takes on different writing styles and pleases the reading and listening public on air and at the various Open mic events. It's a rare combination of fun, dynamic, entertaining and spontaneous yet insightful and thoroughly prepared poetry.

"RAZZMATAZZ" is now available for your reading pleasure at your convenience.

About the Author

Jamaican-born, Creative Entrepreneur, Author, Freelance Writer, Interviewer, Volunteer and Motivational Speaker are some of the 'hats' that Jennifer P. Lumley wears and has also found herself composing radio ads, doing voice-overs and station identification in between her book launches, emceeing, her radio show, The Inspirational Café and Open Mics.

Her work is enjoyed by many from both the Jamaican/Caribbean Diaspora as well as the international audiences. Lumley has grown in cooperative efforts with individuals as well as groups and she entered the arena for the cause of the protection of women and girls on two occasions, collaborating with the African Women's Alliance (AWA) during Women's month (March 2011) in her delivery at the United Nations in New York City.

Lumley is the voice of many through her books, cds, on air, online and traditional local and regional newspaper columns as well as her church's website online 'Prayer of the Week'. She uses her time with better precision than before and is cautiously optimistic at things that appear "too good to be true."

The Author has achieved much despite a few obstacles and some major setbacks. Her close friends think that she is capable of 'making soup from stones'. She relies heavily on one of her favorite philosophers, Rene Descartes whose famous quote "Cogito ergo sum" (I think, therefore I am) keeps her positive and thankful.

Also By Jennifer P. Lumley

Mind Shaper
Faith's Pivotal Role In Altered Cultures

Still Life
Capturing That Special Moment In Time

A Treasury of Prayers
Inspired and Produced by Faith

Our Refuge and Strength
A Sanctuary of Sermons and Prayers

Co-Authored: *"Obstacles & Solutions to African Women's & Girls' Access to Education & Employment"*
(United Nations 2011)

and spoken word CDs

1. SPIRITUAL SELECTIONS
2. POETIC ENCOUNTERS
3. SWEET SWEET JAMAICA
4. THE CHRISTMAS COLLECTION OF POETRY
5. A TREASURY OF PRAYERS (3CD SET)

Dedication

To the Supreme Being; "Bless the Lord O my soul and all that is within me."

To my maternal grandfather, Papa, who had the greatest influence in my life. He bought me my first Bible and helped me to read the 'difficult' words and understand the meaning of the readings, particularly the Psalms. His fine style of dressing I could not help but imitate; he was the constant reminder to me that it is perfectly acceptable to change my mind, "that way I'll keep it clean". Papa taught me the discipline of saving and communicated with me in Spanish as a child and taught me to pass it on. Now my adult daughter has become proficient in Spanish as well. He continued to remind me to travel so that I could "See the world and know the people."

Papa told me innumerable stories and taught me many songs that he learned from his travels to Cuba, Costa Rica and Panama and North America. I still remember them. Thank you Papa…a man well ahead of his times. May Papa's soul find eternal rest as his influence and memories live on.

Acknowledgements

1] The many friends, family members and fellow poets who truly and continually believe in me and have watched me take flight since my first publication. They have been honest and truly helpful in pointing me in the directions they believe would enhance my artistic growth and development. Some have called me late with suggestions to attend or participate in functions; others have called early with excitement about having received a book or a compact disc in the mail and their delight in the progress that I have made. I am sometimes tired but always encouraged. Most of all I consider myself blessed to have them.

2] Rev. Rose Hudson-Wilkin, fellow alumna, (Montego Bay High School, Jamaica) who serves as Chaplain to Her Majesty, Queen Elizabeth among her other roles and who granted me an exclusive interview upon her visit to New York in summer of 2010. The interview prompted me to write a news article, which in turn caught the attention of and several kind and favorable commentaries from other columnists as well as readers.

3] The various persons on radio stations that have aired my work without hesitation and interviewed me because they know the caliber of work and the various themes that I present in my books and on the compact discs. The traditional, as well as the online newspapers, that looked forward to my weekly or monthly delivery of freelance writing and poetry.

4] Maurice's skill to graphically perfect for me, just about anything that I can articulate and make my work complete. Thanks for all that you have taught me to help me to soar.

TABLE OF CONTENTS

RAZZMATAZZ

A Fanfare of Poetry

APART OR TOGETHER

In your absence, I move mountains;
In your presence, we build new worlds.
In my time alone I have reflections;
Together, we rewrite the history of love.

By myself, I gain trust and understanding;
With you, we command total respect.
Separately, we speak strength of character;
Paired, we epitomize a spiritual force of truth.

Unaccompanied, my journey is unique;
Joined and fused, our vision is unparalleled.
Going solo bespeaks rugged endurance;
Our union is the whisper of a delicate intensity.

Jennifer P. Lumley

A RIVETING SPEECH

A riveting speech;
A profound litany;
How wonderfully articulate;
Such moving remarks!!!
What did he mean?
He simply embroidered his oral presentation
With some fancy Bible scriptures
And unusual words.

Suddenly, he is a great orator;
A motivational speaker;
A prolific something-or-another!!!

He strategically grouped his words together
And imposed upon the crowd
When he deployed his conundrum
Calling it elements of speech.

So they all applauded.

But no one understood.

A UNITED STATE

A pinkish, purplish, pumpkin, peach powder-puff,
Fused gold and rusty amber with sandy, coral blush;
Merged dusty apricot, stardust and edible salmon,
Combined pale daffodil with fleshy persimmon.

A sort of terra cotta mingling with papaya flame,
Coalesce into a carroty, summer squash kind of name,
Describing the apricot melt in the pods of bittersweet,
Or maybe tangerine sawdust in the summer heat.

This consortium of honey and vermillion together,
And champagne and tomato on a tangerine feather,
Join the richness of mahogany and tea in gamboge
Resulting in russet elegance and the soft side of a rose.

Yuma blends tangelo, peach blossom and tenne
Mysteriously romantic nostalgia at end of the day;
And a wealthy, unending extravagance of art
Displayed in a gallery when curtain's pulled apart.

This occurrence that results when colors unite
Is a simple indication that day will take flight.
The shades, hues and colors, vivid or just a tinge,
Close daylight's window; night's door on a hinge.

Star dust and gold will soon disappear out of sight;
Though independent, yet united for sight appetite.
Tomorrow again, my hope will be to fill my eyes
With another of God's sunset in the united state of the skies.

Jennifer P. Lumley

BE SEATED, PLEASE

I don't want to sit there,
It's too far in the back.
I'm too close to the kitchen;
Don't give me no flack.

I don't want to sit there,
It's too close to the door.
I might get a draft
Or slip on the floor.

I not sitting there either,
Behind dis ya long column.
Mi cyan hear di people talk;
An mi know seh dem nuh dumb.

Mi nat sittin in the miggle.
Too much talking a tek place.
Disturbance, disturbance everyweh
Right inna yuh face.

An dissa seat yah
Much too close to di speaka box
Boom boom inna yuh earz;
All mi heart staat to knock.

Say what? Excuse me?
I must be seated please?
Before I siddung deh suh,
I kneel dung pon mi knees!

BEYOND FORDHAM

Everybody got off at Fordham. Detraining never seemed so
exciting.
The trained sways to and fro…empty, echoing only the sounds
of the rackety brakes as they rub against the tracks as if
to make them sore from friction.

The air condition swishes and swirls
against the empty and forgotten overhead racks
before chilling the stiff, leatherette seats; row by row; red and blue.
The "NO SMOKING" sign sits old and blurry atop the newest,
metal-framed, cardboard NIKE ad.

No one on the train and yet it moves and rides swiftly
as though hurrying to get someone, late for an appointment,
somewhere. It's lonely except for the company of the tiny
green light that glows with all its might between the elongated,
fluorescent bulbs that dim ever so often and no one knows why.
Maybe it's because everyone got off at the Fordham station.
Happy shoppers. Hoards and hoards of people detrained.
Heads of hair, both long and short, silky and nappy,
coiffed and locked and one just bald and shiny.

They had all left…me and the train to ride
with the conductor and oh yes…
The engineer.

Jennifer P. Lumley

CRIMSON ON WHITE

Fat flakes of snow covered the entire ground;
Snow-capped trees and bushes all around.
A fascinating new world of pristine white;
All eight inches of pure and natural delight.

A Christmas card from my window is what I viewed.
A hypnotic masterpiece with spectacular love imbued.
What a sight; what a beauty; crimson on white;
A cardinal in the snow – an authentic sight.

It feels like a lame attempt to tell you what I envisioned.
Words cannot capture that with much precision.
You had to have been there to see white at its best
And the contrasting magnificence of the cardinal's crimson breast.

CHRYSANTHEMUM

(Walk on stage popping bubble gum)

So,...like, I was ummm, listening to the weather report thingy...
And OMYGAAD...it was like oh so scary, 'cause I didn't know
...aaah if it would rain and stuff on Wednesday. Yasss, Wednesday,
When I wouldda been meetin' up with Chad.
(twist hair around fingers)

Yass, Chad. He kinda like somehow asked me out and I just like,
randomly agreed; but I oh, so don't want it to rain. That way I
could kinda like wear my new FOREVER 21 blouse and my new,
low rise Gap jeans that my mom just like got for me. They are just
so kool, yu know!!!! (pop bubble gum)

So there I was and the phone like rang and rang it just like kept on
ringing...and OMYGADD!!! Guess who's on tha F. O. N. E? It was
Chad, Yass the same Chad we just talked about. He was just like oh
so kool.

He said his first cousin, Chris, was in town so we would have to like
meet, ummm another time. So, but NO...his Mom is an only child
and so is his dad. So like I may be blonde and stuff but I am not
biting that!!!
Well umm, sometimes random people just like show up and say
you're relationship, so anyway. Hmmm. Chris, Christophe, Christina,
Chistopher
Chrysanthymum (pop bubble gum) Did you like hear that big word
I said???
Yass!!! Chrysanthymum!!!
Chris-Aann. Chris-Ann??? That little hot shot cheer leader; she like
OhMyGosh took my Chad. I'll fix her...I'll tell my boyfriend...No I
won't, no I can't. Ok, ok. It's like this.

I'm gonna have my boyfriend tell me when it's not gonna rain and wear my skin tight jeans. I'm gonna like watch the weather channel and like see if I can't spite her and maybe even get like credits for learning something apart from, yuh know, like all the regular school stuff!!!! Watch! I'll fix her.

FIVE NIGHTS AGO

Five nights ago my mind traveled to the place he stayed
And there the baby played
Amongst blood-red poppies.
Happy, as though he knew that Daddy would come home soon.

Five nights ago I blabbed
about my dream.
Five nights later I'm stabbed with the obscene,
the rude and crude interlude of bad news that I now had to chose
the day the ceremony would take place.

My Charlie, my childhood love, my all…had gone;
had gone to war to fight for his country; for those he loved.

Mental meanderings take me to a place where snow does not
settle, but drifts;
where the ocean's gentle tide lifts grains of sand
and you stand
listening to that voice that's no longer there.

We had loved hard, played right, stood tight and always
found a haven in each other's arms.
No arm will do that for me…for Charlie.
My love will be with me and forever stay in the eyes
Of my child even when he's grown and he and I can
share a cup of coffee and talk about
His Dad… My love…
My Charlie.

FOR ANGELETTE

Loving yourself first is what matters most, then you will know how to love others.

Exotic goddess,
Exquisite 'prima donna',
Erotic and phenomenal being,
Eyes twinkling as your smile sparkles.
What foolish manner of man
Would not worship and adore you?
The one who doesn't believe He's good enough for you!
What evil, jealous woman
Would not aim to be your reflection?
The one who sits in a pool
Of discontent with self.
What foolish, young damsel
Would not aspire to mirror your image?
The one too ignorant or unconscious
Yet to comprehend.
They sit restless, ill-at-ease and enraged.
Diva, Empress, Exotic goddess to be admired.
God's child; work so carefully crafted.
Smile and move on with time
With the universe!

FREE AND PRECIOUS

In my wildest dreams
I never would have thought
That angels dwelt on earth;
And appeared without being sought.

They take the form God chooses
And the tasks they must resolve;
Without effort, they're always present,
Free as a wind and full of love.

Precious One. Silent Partner.

Jennifer P. Lumley

FRONT POCKET

You see and know just where to reach
And find your little pen
To write love notes and oaths
To all the pretty women;

And then you take their info too
For nothing's gonna block it.
So sure you'll call for you stand tall
When you secure it in your shirt pocket.

And your old, broken lead pencil
That leaves marks on your vest,
Is slipped right underneath it,
In that pocket against your chest.

Without looking or even trying to aim,
You're sure it's always there;
That faithful, dirty shirt pocket
Has already had its fair share.

You poke it and you push it,
Never wondering if there is a rip,
Or a tiny hole or a big gap,
Through which your little pen could slip.

It sits there and gathers dust
While you are so busy struttin'
Never ever wondering what you would do
If that pocket should go rotten.

Tissues used when you have a cold,
Guess where that tissue goes?
Deep down in your front pocket,
See, now everybody knows!

You treat that shirt pocket so bad,
It just sits and gathers lint
But regardless of all of that
You can still find yourself fresh mint.

You see the way you treat your shirt pocket
That's just how you treat your women;
You stuff her with all kinds of things.
Back up now…just hold on all you men!!!

Try wearing another shirt one day;
Maybe one with no shirt pocket.
Try finding someplace else to plug it;
Try not to use this socket.

See how it feels to do without?
Now try again a shirt with a pocket.
You treat it well and you will see
That a woman won't try to block it.

15

GIRLZ NIGHT OUT

The shortest skirts, the highest heels
A balancing act, a thrill to feel.
The tightest dress, a glass of wine,
Shiny lip gloss; this night is divine.
The cutest styles, the latest fashions;
Boys smile and look on with a passion.
Bathed, blushed, coiffed and drowned in perfume
Cigarette smoke fills up the room
Music thomps interspersed with giggles
As you dance and prance, and jump and wiggle.
Said that he touch you, on your soft shoulder?
His muscles ripple under his shirt like a boulder.

Before the midnight hour ladies enter for free.
Boys come out in great numbers, the ladies to see.
It's a lavish party where everyone should be;
It's a razzmatazz thing; it's a jamboree.
Tight jeans, neat haircuts, clean and shiny shoes.
Neat moustache, he's cute just singing the blues.
Ladies glow and men perspire after much dancing
Out comes the handkerchief for facial enhancing
Drinks for girls are on the house; now isn't that sweet?
Truly it's like a dream; it's a wonderful treat.
Next Thursday I'll be back and I'm gonna shout it out
There's nothing quite as groovy as a "GIRLZ NIGHT OUT".

Jennifer P. Lumley

HEAR YOUR INNER VOICE

The noise of the world can drown your inner voice.

You do want to hear it. It's important that you do.

You have to listen long enough.

You must be still.

HOURGLASS IN THE HAMPER

As I face the Saturday morning cleaning,
I see mounds of dishes and piles of laundry.
I try to choose which job gets done first
Since the house is in total disarray.

To keep a completely, tidy house
Is really a mammoth task
And I don't have a magic wand
But I have something in that flask.

The dusty floors beckon me
With little piles of hairs and dust.
The mirror shows only partial images
Attend to this, I must.

The dishes sit and seem to stare;
Come now! No, no more stress.
From the overflowing laundry basket,
I'll start off with this pretty, little dress.

This limp, jumbled heap of clothing
I place in their logical order and piles;
This crushed batch of crumbled formation
Whites and colors are all my child's.

It may seem odd that I relish
This task that spurs me on
To accomplish even greater tasks
Once I have begun.

You see there's a certain secret
When you put things in order
And make them clean once again
With a fresh scent to savor.

Colorful pants and pajamas,
Undershirts, socks and skirts,
Embroidered, pretty panties,
Wash cloths, sweat suits and shirts.

Have you ever sat and watched that machine
How the collection of colors just spin?
Seems like a bouquet of flowers;
Pink, purple, turquoise, yellow and green.

All garments and towels have a blast
And bring such great delight.
Stains all removed; Yes, Shout it out.
My whites are once again white.

The passing years have run away;
The Smurfs and My Little Pony have fled.
Strawberry Shortcake was her favorite;
Book bag, socks and the canopy for her bed.

Coordinating those pretty clothes
That hugged the body of my child,
Is something to which I've looked forward
Though I know it might sound wild.

But the hourglass fills up as the hamper
And I try to grab on to the tails
Of those pleasant years and memories
And laundry in piles and bails.

I can feel the warmth of the blanket
Caressing me as it leaves the dryer;
A few strands of hair on the pillowcase;
The hourglass is no liar.

Yes, these are some of the simple things
That my lovely daughter brought to my life,
So with gratitude for the abundance of her love
And her laundry, I say "I'm a happy housewife".

HUMBLE, HAPPY BIRTHDAY

Dinner napkins on the table;
Four course meal, well prepared
With cutlery shining brightly
And stomachs empty and bare
For the long-promised meal
Looking very delicious.
Taste buds are busy;
It's actually quite sumptuous.

The salad is perfect;
Greens, oranges and reds.
'Tatoes, pork chops and broccoli,
Fit for a king to be fed.
With just enough spices
And seasons for flavor
Though you want to swallow fast
You must chew slowly to savor.

Hmm hmm hmm taste that love,
Look at the presentation!
You almost don't want to touch or taste
But you'll miss the palate sensation.
Great ambiance for dining,
It's real, it's not fake.
Then SURPRISE & HAPPY BIRTHDAY!
Here is your birthday cake.

I AIN'T SO HAPPY TODAY

Don't nobody want your man.
An Honey, you betta be glad.
Don't nobody want a broke down house,
'Cause that just ain't the fad.

Don't nobody want his broke-up self
And breath stinking with liquor;
Don't know one want that worn out dude;
His lights won't even flicker.

No. Everybody wants to shine real bright;
And to stand out among the rest;
An' drive in dem real fancy cars and stuff.
I must just have the very best.

Your ole man ain't hardly movin';
Stares hard and then he stutta,
Like he tryin' to rev up his engine
But all you hear is ffflutta, ffflutta.

Who know what he be talking 'bout,
Or what he be trying to say.
Don't nobody want that ole drunken fool
That gambled his life all away.

(pause then look left and right)
Honey, be happy no one wants him.
Keep him; yes, let him stay.

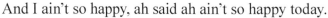

My man done gone with a young wench
And I ain't so happy, ah said ah ain't so happy today.

Jennifer P. Lumley

I'M GETTING OLD, OLD MAN

How long did it take you, Old man please tell me how long,
How long it took to have your brow so perfectly furrowed?
And eyes that squint against the bright sunlight,
With equally rhythmic force?

Old man with arthritic fingers bent toward the horizon,
And nails jaundiced with age;
Teeth criss-crossed and cracked, others missin'.
Old man how come you smile so easily,
As though you say 'hakuna matata',
Your problem free philosophy – hakuna matata.

Your smooth bald head seems shiny and lacquered;
Only age could make it so;
No hairs dare grow or show.
Old man when will you tell me?
How long will it take before you tell me old man?
How long did it take to get your shoes bent, pigeon-toed,
Dry and etched with creases for your comfort?

Tell me please old man, because I'm busy getting old,
Just waiting for you to utter those few and simple words.
How come you are so patient and yet you are sooo oold?
Everyone seems to know you and wave at chya
As though you are a king or a movie star…
Wise, old man, there is none as old as you!
Old man in your world, aren't you alone?

Jennifer P. Lumley

IN A LAND OF MEN

In a land of men
a land all their own,
women wait in line after line;
in formation waiting to be called
to get information on how
to change their maiden names,
in a land ruled by men.
In a land of men where there is lack,
Of women; woe men, woe;
where scarcity exists
and is the order of the day,
women wait close to you.
In a land of men.

INDIGO CHILD

On the go…Indigo
Indigo…not blue, not lilac
Indigo!!!
Not purple, no not violet.
Sits comfortably in between;
Grouped but distinct,
On the color spectrum
A tincture
In your own style,
Indigo Child.
Intuitive and Spiritual.

Essence of cyan and magenta
Gentle in nature
Full of zest and
Indigo warm.
Liberated, soft aura
A captivating
Indigo charm.
And thirty two Indigo petals
Point downward;
Indigo Child of laughter and love
You are different.
Royalty.
Indigo, You are.

Jennifer P. Lumley

I'VE BEEN CALLED AN AWE-FULL WOMAN

Yes I am an awe-full woman. I've been called that before.
Admiration and fear I can cause, though I have never roared.
The gentlest words I'll utter, as warm love becomes awe-full fire;
Awe-full is not a bad word at all, when used as an intensifier.

Amazing it is to you, how I managed with three kids
And no financial support I got, respectfully, however, I did.
I am an awe-full woman. I cause feelings of terror;
Of dread mixed up with wonder; yet a gentle smile in the mirror.

Those deep abiding qualities, of politeness and respect,
Are the traits by which I live and never will neglect.
I will not bend and fold for you, or bad habits you may adopt
And mis-educate my children, such that poverty will be their lot.

I'm such an awe-full woman, my children understand;
Don't possibly try to hurt them, or your friendship will be banned.
My flesh, my blood, my body, my nine month wear and tear;
Dismiss the thought of hurting them; keep living in awful fear.

I am an awe-full woman and awe-fully interesting too;
And awe-fully energetic and awe-fully tried and true.
I'm full of awe-fully new ideas and awe-fully creative thoughts;
And always awe-fully helpful, 'cause I was awe-fully, well-taught.

I am usually awe-fully well-dressed from crown to tippy toes;
My presence is revered from a distance; you will never get close.
Yes, a woman of awe I am, usually walking with God alone;
My God is oh so awesome; He's with me while on His throne.

I am the sister you want to have or the mother of your young;
The carefree qualities you have seen while I hum and sing along.
The neighbor you so well deserve; the friend filled with awe.
Still in wonderment you gaze, on this phenomenal je ne sais quoi.

I'VE MADE UP HIS MIND

Yes, I can.
I can see the child's complexion now.
His and mine together...as one...beautiful.
He's smooth; velvety smooth and dark like rich chocolate.
Look at the muscle tone; his structure – athletic, chiseled representation!!!
He glides across the room and heads turn though he is not the best looking man,
But I've made up his mind, since he is always so busy thinking and doing...not ever knowing.

Such strength of character is depicted in his jaw line and his cheekbone.
The wooly hair sits on his head like a Mandingo...got the picture?
Never smiling; always methodically calculating the next move and the few words uttered are carefully and deliberately chosen.

Can he be mine? My man? Mine alone? Just imagine! My Huuusband!!!
I am Mrs. HIM, whatever his name is.
Here's the deal. I WANT HIM...and I won't try, 'cause that's how you lose 'em.
The subject is well schooled. Solid, white teeth; nails like nails oughta be and long lashes too. Great bone structure ; tall and lean without an ounce of fat.
I don't know him...yet, but I will get to know him...intimately...in time.

I've made up his mind...he will love me. He's perfect.
I've made up my mind...he is.

I WAKE UP EVERY MORNING

I wake up every morning with a hunger;
A hunger to do good;
A hunger to know more;
A hunger that won't leave my being
And will not let me rest
Until I have a better understanding
Of the inequalities and the injustices of this world.

I wake up every morning.
I keep on waking up with great expectations.
I woke up one September morn
Plagued with great perplexities.
Troy Davis, a man who hungered for life
and not for his last meal;
Troy Anthony Davis, a man about to be put to death, prays.
Prays for the souls of those who will administer
His lethal injection.
I wake up every morning.
This is not a dream.

JUST ONCE MORE

I know you know I love you and I don't say it often enough and stuff; but Babe, I know you undastand the deal. So one day I'm gonna show you my appreciation; but see, things can get kinda tough when ya husslin an yu just wanna get home alive. You know what I'm talkin' 'bout right?

It's wild in the streets Babe, wilder than ever; and now with another child on the way...howd'ya let that happen? Whyd'ya do that to me Babe? I'm gonna love you once more for good Babe and it's for sure. 'Cause I trust ya. We'll try once more to keep the family together and one day get an apartment that's big enough. Let me try just once more to show you my love and tell you that I love you.

See when a man's gotta juggle and stuff, feelings get mixed up and sometimes even lost when things are rough. Man, it's like so easy to criticize you and find all your faults, like I was built faultless! It's easier than buying you flowers or complimenting you...so just once more, give me the chance to prove that I'm a man and live up to my word because right now, that's all I'm down to...my word. I can't afford to lose that.

Babe, if you must know, I'll tell you just once more, that I love you; I love you; I really do. You what's funny Babe? It's getting easier to say, now that I done said it just once more!

KING MAN

Impeccable speech,
You tried and reached.
You never gave up.
I loved you before long.
I made you my King Man.
And man you are a king!!!
Royalty, crowned;
Noble and majestic.
You take the time to be fantastic.
You provide sweet kisses for my taste buds;
Warm hugs for my tired being;
Soft words to caress my ears;
Gentle entertainment and THEN,
Three beautiful children.
Your deliberate choice,
To carry on your voice
And strong African lineage.
Imperial. All standing strong
On their individual pedestals.
King man, you made me Queen!!!

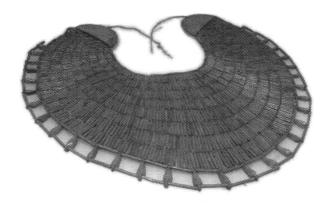

Jennifer P. Lumley

KLIPPITY KLOP

Klippity klop, kutty kop kutty kop;
I met a boy and he's hot, hot, hot.
He's hot, yes he's hot, that's what I said;
Klippity klop klop, he's hot is what I said.

My heart skips a beat, then another real fast,
When this hot boy speaks or just walks past
My doorway; in my mind it's a test;
Oh my klippity klop gosh; my heart won't rest.

It's happening, I klippity klop knew it would
So doggone nice and real klipptiy klop good
Snap, bang, kaboom, there it goes again.
He's excessively fabulous; it's kutty kop insane.

Klippity help klop me klippity klop help me
I klippity klop want him to klippity klop me
I'm in love, klippity klunk, let me fall in his arm;
'Cause I'm slurpy klippity kloppity sure it's warm.

Klippoty klop kaboom, kitty kop kutty kop
My heart's racing for this klippity boy hot.
WHOOOOSH!!!!

LET'S SUPPOSE

Suppose, now just suppose,
You had hair that had no tension;
Hair that hung way down your back;
Not a wig or an extension.

Then suppose, now just suppose,
You had a perfect body form;
One that suited you just right
And fitted the societal norm.

And suppose, now let's suppose,
You had that hmm hmm GQ man,
Who worshipped and adored you,
Making all those 'just-right' plans.

Now suppose, again let's suppose,
Some children came along;
And in this union all went well,
Everything was right - nothing wrong.

So suppose, let's again, suppose,
You bought and won the lottery;
Acquired new friends and neighbors,
Expensive paintings; exotic pottery.

Critical mass has been achieved.
Things longed for, safely ensconced.
Suddenly gone from throne to gutter.
Sin-spiration now criss-crossed.

Now suppose, a big suppose,
You woke up and it were a dream.
Suppose for a moment you had no one.
You alone made up your team.

Jennifer P. Lumley

Your hair needs a relaxer,
Jimmy naps won't leave your head.
Your perfect body was simply a wish;
The man, a body-pillow in bed.

You realize your neighborhood
Is all the very same
No big plans; no change at all;
You still use your maiden name.

The lottery number you should have bought
Or even placed a bet,
Reminds you that things are the same;
And you are still deep in debt.

LIME LIFE

Hunched over, under the burden of weight
Of limes in a basket, picked early in the morning
While all else were asleep.
Trudging along to sell every single, hard, green lime;
Limes that are green, even when they are ripe.

You won't know her cares looking at her countenance.
She doesn't beg or ask for favors except...
Begging her children not to wave, not to say hello;
Not to even to act as though they recognize her
As they walk pass her with their troop of friends
And her, with her basket of limes...bitter limes.

An oath taken not to embarrass her children...
An edict to make sure they are educated
From those limes; sour, green limes;
And in a better place than that in which they were born;
Not one, not two but all three of them, promising;
Sworn to make sure that they don't lime.

Her frame, like the lime, is small but hard and
Refreshingly excited with flavor.
Her faith in God will move her children...
Will bring awareness and shape their minds,
From a basket of limes...caustic, bitter limes.

Who will buy them is not her concern,
Rather, how quickly can she sell them so she can
Return home and make the dresses for the daughters
In the church choir and a vest for the son in the marching band.
What time will it be when she garners sufficient funds
To provide dinner and feed her young ones?
In the present, she doesn't ask what time it is;

Jennifer P. Lumley

Her vision is an arrow shot into the future.
What time will it be when self sacrifice pays off?
When a harvesting song will be sung with pride?
What time will the under-privileged become?

She breaks the rules and does not wait for the village
To raise her children; but life has a way of creating
This wonderful balance, by squeezing juicy pulp;
By providing fresh water and sweeeeet sugar
To make a cool drink of lime-ade;
And in the summer, sip it with cold cubes of ice.

'Summer time and the livin' is easy....' [Sung as you smile and walk
away.]

LISTEN WITH AN ACCENT

You did not invite me to this country;
I came of my own free will.
It's not the only country I'd visited
But I made it my home and I'm here still.

And you know after almost forty years,
So many people keep saying the same thing:
"Oh I hear a kind of lilt in your speech"
"An unidentifiable accent, with a nice ring".

Once I spent quite some time giving a woman
Some professional financial advice.
She smiled and asked me to repeat everything;
The lady heard nothing but said she loved my voice.

Sometimes when they look at me and listen,
I'm described as the fair-skinned Black girl,
With an unusual English last name, prim and proper,
And a vocabulary from out of this world.

I'm from this very same world as you;
I'm just from the tropical part.
The place that has the white sand beaches,
That refreshes your mind, soul and heart.

I'm from the 'no problem' country;
The reggae beat and 'whaapen man' land.
I'm quite able to articulate the Queen's English,
Den switch back again to 'yeah man'.

And when I came to this country.
I really had to strain my ears to hear
The assorted and varied pronunciations.
You have to listen with a clean, keen ear.

Not because you are from these parts,
Believe it or not, you also have an accent.
Some are distinctly from the South
Northerners, are, in contrast, are quite different.

I used to say she-dule where I'm from,
Here, it is called your SKEDULE
We're talking about the very same thing
What I call an ass you may call a fool.

I've had to re-learn the spelling of words
Such as center, theater, honor and endeavor
A c.h.e.c.k. for me once was once c.h.e.q.u.e.
Those spelling ties I've had to sever.

It's really not so complicated at all
To carry on any meaningful conversation.
Don't get caught up or bogged down with accents
Or cause any linguistic complication.

See if you can do like me,
Having arrived in a distant land so different.
Listen carefully to hear and comprehend.
Learn to listen with an accent!!!

LOVE FOCUS

Lies, screaming lyz;
Butterflyz in the skyz and
Lascivious desirez
Dream aflame cryz.
Delivery from tyz
To more exciting liez.
Pleasant insanity dyz
As heavenly pain sighz;
Loving feeling viez
Against time that fliez.
Awaken now; c'mon rize.
Focus on your love; be wize.

LOVE'S INSTRUCTIONS

Life and love are the encounters of this earth that sometimes are manifest only when looked at again and again if you ever get the chance. Long walks, open, honest communication, birthdays and anniversaries, new babies and a celebration of life for every reason God put on earth and for no reason - that's the foundation of our love. Just great!

With prayers and supplications to God, in conjunction with careful evaluation, several opinions from medical personnel and the corporate decision by the family, this life and this love had to be looked at, again.

A young girl with zest, celebrating life with her friends – too much, just a little too much, had now found herself in a body cast in the same hospital as my wife, who was now on life support with little or no chance of ever recovering…except as a being… hardly being. Two worlds crossing…clashing, crashing.

Try mustering up the courage to do the superb job that she would expect according to her driver's license – DNR. DO NOT RESUSCITATE. It seems plain, straight-forward and simple. I would want to go in a dignified manner. I would want to go and not linger for more than a week-max!!! It had been more than that, yet this terrible albatross hung around my neck like the ancient mariner; with water everywhere and not a drop to drink; her instructions were there and I could not follow through.

When you hang on to the hope of love and life like that which we built, you must look again and reflect…but you must do it. It is your obligation without looking or feeling atilt.

Without true love we just exist. It is my true love that has brought me to this point. I have decided. I can live with that.

Jennifer P. Lumley

MARRIAGE MYTHOLOGY

Engaged in a manner that's understood
Only by those who have been engaged.
Not to be married but to become occupied
In the other's exchange of thoughts and ideas;
Reflections and memories of most things
Pleasant and orderly.

Herculian task involved in remaining uninvolved;
Enjoying your separateness; a challenge beyond
Measure not to want to go further...and marry
But tarry so as not to go to Hades.

Muse you must, so Cupid will not shoot his arrow
Of love through the aortic valves; but failing that
You then become narcissistic finding your true
Beauty. Otherwise, you may have to climb
Mount Olympus in order not to be condemned
Like Atlas.

Married but single...bearing the weight
Of the world on your shoulders...alone!

Jennifer P. Lumley

MI PELO SOLITARIO
(My Lonely Hair)

From one little follicle on the side of my shin
Lo and behold there was something thin
Laying comfortably on my epidermis.
I wondered to myself "Now what is this?"

I used my hand and tried to brush it away
But it sat steadfast and it decided to stay.
When did it arrive, unbeknownst me
This inch-long black hair, oh golly gee!

Originally I thought it was a piece of thread
And when I yanked on it I knew it wasn't dead.
Me oh my! That hair felt so soft and silky
Against my skin so smooth and milky.

Though by itself could not insulate me from the cold
This inch-long black hair was without bend or fold
It will not be shaved, dyed, plucked, waxed, cut or trimmed;
My lonely hair lying comfortably on the side of my shin.

It's not a beard or sideburns since it's not on my face
It's like the lone ranger with style, class and grace;
It's not like a fiber or thread, or hair or a pin.
It's my lonely, inch-long, hair on the side of my shin.

MISS JAMAICA/US SILVER JUBILEE

Let them doubt you if they want to,
Let them criticize, if they must or dare;
Let them stand in awe and wonder;
Let someone, in you, place their trust and care.

Their walk is not quite like your stride.
Their smile does not have your warmth.
Their look is not quite like your countenance.
You're serene with an unmatched calm.

You were chosen for your good looks and style,
Your charm, your intellect, your personality;
Your potential to always be poised and confident,
Showing civility, compassion and congeniality.

I'm sure you have big visions for the world;
And you are certainly an agent of change;
Whether it's in the arts or in astrophysics,
The future depends on those in your age range.

Absorb all you can in this process today;
It may be your one and only chance
To form some lifelong and true friendships,
As in your years, you advance.

Ladies, follow through with your many dreams and goals.
Put specific, measureable action plans in place;
Time your realistic achievements and ask questions.
Run your own race and do it with style and grace.

I crown you all as queens, champions and winners;
Your quirky little ways make you so much fun.
You are witty and cordial; you are an absolute delight.
Beauties vying for the title of "Miss Island in the Sun".

Jennifer P. Lumley

MISS-TERIOUS

You've entered my mind in a most mysterious way, to once again find that you can't linger or stay. Fair dame, mystical creature rare, not obvious to ordinary intelligence, unravel the strings of my heart and let me do my part to keep my peace of mind.

Your outward, visible appearance sends me reeling down the spiral of discontent, thirsting while bursting for more of the same. My heart palpitates as your presence causes such mental commotion.

Stay lady; be mine. Oh lass divine play the harpsichord of love. Maiden be reminded that my whole being is disturbed and yet absorbed simultaneously by the disorderly outbursts of emotions. The tumult in my veins wreak havoc.

Your presence in my brain makes me believe that you have seeped into my soul and taken up residence like a scofflaw, causing uproar and kerfuffle.

This is not just a dream. This is love.

Jennifer P. Lumley

$$ MONEY POEM $$

A $pecial piece of paper,
With a $eal and $ignatures too
And $erial numbers on both ide,
Make me think of you.

Each note ha$ a pre$ident,
All of whom are dead.
Without some of these 'dead bills',
Many people will not wed.

It makes a good impre$$ion
And affords a certain lifestyle
But if not spent with utmost care,
Will last for only a short while.

My bill, my buck, my booty,
Happy cabbage, dollar green, my stash,
My juice, my dough, my nest egg,
Are only a few names for CA$H!!!

MUZIK MAN

You have a certain style, a style that's all your own,
That pleases the listening public on a Sunday afternoon.
When your program on the radio begins
They laugh, they cry, they love they sin;
Quietly remembering their first loves
Sharing life like two turtle doves.
Sweet-bitter love is sometimes a part
Of what you bring to a true LOVER'S heart.

You see, love is never complete bliss
But music man, folks think of their first kiss.
Old time rhythm, authentic beat,
Music to sing to or rock on your feet;
Love songs galore, reggae sweet and smooth,
Rastaman chant and symphonies to groove.
Pleasing, harmonious medicine for the soul.
Lyrics and lines; hot warm and cold.

Truthfully music man, every Sunday's operation
Brings artistic, auditory sensation,
Incorporating an instrumental voice banner;
A structured, continuous, euphonic manner.
You have a message to tell and many ears to please
Your music prevents and alleviates any Dis-Ease.
Mi amigo, No te preocupe. Grazie!
Music man, thank you, muchas gracias, merci.

Jennifer P. Lumley

ONE, TWO, THREE...GREEN LIGHT

The cell phone, fully charged, is one;
The VCR has one, that makes two;
My mini cell tower has three in one;
My copier-scanner-fax has a green light too.

Is this what they call "Going Green"?
Lying in bed with the electric blanket,
Its control housed secretly in a white cover but shows
A window with the green gauge that glows
Because it also wants to be seen.

One, two, three and more, many more green lights
At night
Distracting you as you make
That other attempt to go to sleep...
Eyes burning from their glare in the thick darkness,
Pitch blackness so dense, so heavy, so aged.

And the intruder, interfering with rest.
No longer do I count sheep.
At best,
I better cover my head,
Cozy up to that body pillow and pray
for sleep,
after one, two, three...green lights.

OTHER'S DAY

This Sunday is Mothers' Day
And we celebrate it all day long
But not everyone was happy
For many it was worrisome
Because some women don't have children
Or they do but not a good relationship.
So we take time out today with
All due respect to Mothers' Day
And would like to celebrate this time
And call it "Other's Day".

Jennifer P. Lumley

OUR REAL PRIORITY

Yuh tip up inna spike heel, yuh red-up red-up yuh two lip;
Yuh bat yuh yeye dem faas-faas; yuh swing an sway yuh hip.
Every drum beat, yuh run gawn, wearing di lates' fashion;
Yuh drown yusself inna perfume; yuh sip wine wid yuh gang.

Yuh tink any of dese tings mek yuh a complete ooman?
Yuh really believe it help yuh? Stop and tink bout it nuh man.
Yuh nuh educate yusself, or go learn wan trade a school.
So yuh cyan teach yuh pickney dem. Now yuh an dem fool-fool.

Yuh nuh stap fi cook a prappa meal; yuh always eating on the run.
Yuh tyad out yusself a night time, a day time yuh nuh get nuh sun.
It bad wen yuh bun out yusself but nuh ruin these young minds!!!
Dis next generation is PRIORITY. Observe di waaning signs.

Saggin pants below dem batty; blouse cut deep inna dem chess;
Tun roun di wud saggin; yuh nah go like a wah yuh a go get.
A dem a go run dis country in jus a few shaat years.
Mi 'fraid fi even think 'bout it; but me nah tap say my prayaz!!!

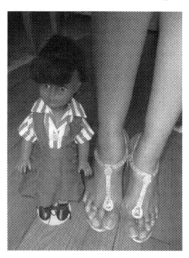

PIZZAZZ AND RAZZMATAZZ

Here's that funky little poem
That'll make you jump and jig
And do the hustle or the waltz
Or the belly dance that you dig.

Sporty midriff, rhythmic rumba
An Afro, some sequins and pleats
Jive on a cloud in your jipijapa
Or keep the country and western beat.

Paso doble, bossonova,
Hiphop, ballroom and tango;
Slip on the fedora and dashiki
Get high with the sweet flamenco.

That red beret fits you just fine.
Fly like the jitterbug or even ballet.
Quite suitable for the salsa as well,
As the foxtrot, swing and meringue.

Rock with the reggae music beat;
Sink deep in the culture mix.
Swing to and fro with the calypso,
Now the generation gap is fixed.

So whether you chose tie-dye or batik
Or disco, tap or some jazz,
As an old timer or modern dancer
We know you have pizzazz and razzmatazz.

POETIC PANACHE

Teach me your poetry,
C'mon teach me your style;
I'm willing to learn it,
C'mon teach me your style.

Is it easy to remember, or is it hard to forget?
Is it jazzy, kinda rhyming; smooth and somewhat wet?
Does it have its own sweet rhythm?
Thunders its own beat?
Will it make you jump up and down
Or just sit down in your seat,
Trying to remember
Each and every line;
And how you pitched your voice
Or kept it sublime?

Teach me your poetry,
C'mon teach me your song;
Does it have its own peculiar name?
Or should I just sing along?

Oh how I like your poetry;
No, no I won't forget the intonations and the quietness;
I'm caught up in your net.

I comprehend it all and trying to make it work.
I'm saturated with your rhythm and filled with the perk.
My intuition tells me that I need to do it with a difference.
I do need my own pulsations and electric, recurring waves.
Mine must be bold, without reason or explanation;
Intense, graphic and vivid; my lyrics will be a sensation.

I need my own lyrics, my own distinct set of words;
My own style, my panache, my direction and moods.
I must be able to fit in the groove and to move the crowd
With a language that transcends all barriers,
Brings a hush to the baby's cry, comforts the old man's sigh;
Compliments the beauty of the countryside and mountains high.

Teach me your poetry because it's not mine.
I'll teach you what I have learnt from you in vogue,
Then it becomes all thine.

Jennifer P. Lumley

PRO-TEEN FOR KNEE-GROW

Pro-teen, yes it means I am for the teens;
To live up to their potential and pull up their jeans;
Take that walk, lose weight and be sun kissed and well.
Put down the remote, the Sunkist soda, and hell,
Wake up out of that dream;
Although it is a necessary sleeping disorder,
Or wake up in a cell and face some faulty truths.
Flex your muscles of faith; or face that brute.
Was it just your fate served to you in a cup?
Why settle DOWN when you can settle UP?
The Power of LOVE is different from the love of power.
Go green, stay green and stand tall like a tower.
Weed will make you stumble. Anything for the migrane?
Protein for the brain; drugs to drive you insane.
Your gang's your feet fleet and gets the drug movin'
But if the timing isn't right the outcome won't be grovin'.
Who has time to buy broken peas?
Valentino; No valentine dances with the trees.
I lost mine so now I have retired; or have I been retried?
Smiles across the miles interrupt my being;
Throws off my balance and stability;
Keeps me in a pivotal role,
Although interfering with my equilibrium.
Choices are yours. Be a WINNER or a WHINER.
Get it done. The job is yours.
The stinking little voice inside of you
Is outside of someone else. Do the math.
Don't add up what they're trying to say.
In math you add and add to infinity;
In life you add and add to insanity.
I am pro-teen.
Stressed? Hell no. Look at it backwards.
Now it is D E S S E R T S!!! Right, Desserts.

You are on a roll.
Get to know a sleepin' policeman;
Regain with Rogain,; yup you are getting old teen.
Little Negro. Don't let them call you that.
Well how else and what else and…well?
Knee Grow, feet, grow, hands grow.
Use your brain and go ONE STEP BEYOND
Remember that show? Nah, U R too young
But you can go BEYOND STEP ONE.
These are not Soul Train days;
It's a Foul Train that lays waiting to haul you off
Don't sit down, or hang out.
Steps are hard and bullets get you wet with blood,
Running red…and warm…and non-stop…till you die
Or cry for your Mama who taught you what she knew.
It wadd'n much. You sit in the Rough Work Column.
N E G R O watching your knee grow;
Swollen from beatings.
One more serving of love; perhaps
If Bubba decides.
Now you want to pull up your pants!!!
I am Pro-Teen
You can do anything you want;
But can you live comfortably with the consequences of that decision?
I am Pro-Teen.
I cannot walk on water.
I can write an epileptic epic
I have awakened out of a coma.
Now I am a MIND SHAPER,
LIFE CHANGER,
A MOVER AND A SHAKER.
CHANGE MAKER
When you hear that it cannot be done, it's usually an interruption from you getting it done.

Jennifer P. Lumley

REAL GREEN

Exhaust, more exhaust;
Air exhausted with pollutants
From the trucks and buses
And yes the cars.
The Bimmer and the Benz
Come out with frenx then
Your air is polluted and exhausted
From the process.

Hop on the train;
Use the rail, it's not in vain.
That compost is a garden insulator;
Keeps the garden fresh both now and later.
Ever heard of bamboos?
Then use some.
It consumes air born carbon
And makes new, fresh air faster
Than other plants do.

Trust 'cause we have to.
Solar power, wind power, energy conservation;
Change that shower head - make it a conversation.
Shut down electronics;
Wash clothes in cold water;
Swap books, don't buy new ones…again.
You can power up a TV for a full three hours
From one recycled aluminum can.

Light bulbs…eureka!
This is incandescent;
Save some more energy
With the fluorescent.
C'mon all. This is just the beginning,
I'm just telling you to be environmentally responsible.

RETURNED...

It's not every day that we find

A friend way back from thirty years;

It's not uncommon that after meeting,

That parting won't have tears.

So as you continue to journey along

And travel on life's unexpected road,

Remember for the next thirty years

Or more, your heart's in my abode.

SATTA MASSAGANA
[Amharic Language Spoken In Ethiopia]

Phenomenal Woman, Daughter, Sister and Mother;
Lover of outdoor activity and restaurants, like Father.
Relentless and Powerful, Pioneer and Trend-setter;
Marching to the beat of any drum; you Jet-setter.

You are a Practical, Determined, Strong-willed Soul;
Your Resilience and Care promotes your Motherly Role.
As a Sister, you are Genial, Helpful, Inspiring and Sharing;
As a daughter you're a Cultured Perfectionist and Caring.

Friends remember Purple as your Color of Preference;
Lilac sometimes is also a Good Point of Reference.
It's the Color of Meditation, Creativity, Imagination and Mystery;
It bespeaks Royalty and connects you to Universal Sources of
Energy.

Lovey, Princess, Jenikinz, JENNAY ALEXIS BARRETT.
You have a Sense of Purpose and you know how to carry it.
Phenomenal Friend, Woman. Daughter, Sister and Mother,
Focused and Balanced. You're a delight to both Father and Mother.

HAPPY EARTH DAY

GIVE THANKS AND PRAISE. SATTA MASSAGANA.

Jennifer P. Lumley

SERVICE MAID OR SERVICE-MADE

I've had a few of them in my life
But does it really matter?
Some were tall and some were thin,
A few were fat and others fatter.

Some were severe in their treatment.
A few of them were really strict;
Others I recall were soft-spoken
And not too busy with the lip.

I've had one or two to embrace me
Complimented my performance and my ways.
To several of them I didn't really matter;
They just wanted to get through the days.

There were those who took the time out
To be deliberately well-dressed,
With a pleasant countenance that I liked
I was impressionable, I must confess.

They've all left an indelible etching in my life;
On my mind are the imprints they have marked.
My teachers were different but they all made a contribution
To the life journey on which I've embarked.

SWEET SONGBIRD, YOU HAVE SUNG

In memory of Whitney Elizabeth Houston – unmatched in her vocal prowess. (1963 – 2012)

Unencumbered now!!!
Free after you have *exhaled*.
Cease breath from restless tides,
For *one moment in time*,
Recognizing the *greatest love of all*.

We sing your songs but our efforts cannot
Be compared to your vocal prowess;
We cannot attain that perfect pitch,
Nor can we unveil the mystery
Of your brief, beautiful existence.
Our dreams we dare not trust
For fear of the hidden gate to eternity.

How can we now regret that you have left
Your fragmented aloneness and scattered suffering
To join the heavenly choir? Your touch still lingers.
As family, we embrace your open, trusting heart
A heart that unfolded and accepted
Love's *joy* and pain.
Yet you sang through the winters
Of your grief,
Remedied your soul in the Summers
Of silence and tranquility.

Numbered and known are the grains of sand
Much like the hairs on our heads
And in God's infinite power
He counted you too and named you like the
Stars in the heavens – *Whitney Elizabeth Houston*.
And He said *"I will always love you"*.

Jennifer P. Lumley

Nippy, you were chosen to **shine**
And you were guided to **sparkle**.
Your day of parting
Became a day of gathering...
And we say THANKS.

Now go. Enjoy your well-deserved, eternal rest!

SONGBIRD OF THE CENTURY

You have been the sweetness in my tea;
You have been more than good to me;
And when the world began to see your face
Your smile, your charm your style, your grace
And hear the big voice from little Whitney,
They started to better understand
The spice of life; the salt of the land.

You were everyone's gift and company
At home, in the car and at the party.
My dancing partner that they couldn't see;
My soul no longer shy because of you Whitney.
I sang in the shower, my mike was the soap.
And like fresh flowers, you brought me hope.
A new look at life; a new way to cope.

You are that perfect curl on a bad hair day;
The exquisite jewelry on my neck on display;
The warm smile of both my neighbors and friends
And warm summer breeze that never ends.
You are the kind, loving words in a greeting card.
You were my songbird and my bodyguard.

Every girl was a woman and every woman a girl
Because of you songbird, we became one world;
And every musical note that you ever perfected
Became reason for another song to be selected
As a winner for a Grammy and a time to celebrate
All the reasons for love and no time for hate.

Each time your lips parted, each note that you kissed
Each melody you sang brought everyone such bliss
Because the notes had come out to decorate the earth
With happiness and joy and value and worth;
And you sang and praised God in high notes and low
And again we all knew you were the entire show.

You have warmed the cockles of everyone's hearts.
In the secret portals of our minds you had your parts.
Your beauty was the ornament on our Christmas tree.
You still mean a great deal to the world and to me.
You sang and praised God in all places of His dominion,
With happiness you did so with rhythm circadian

Whitney, you came and you played your part.
Now earth you have left, to heaven you depart
To sing as always in this new role you start
Sing on, cherished one.
Sweet Songbird, you are still everyone's sweetheart.

THAT DOG

I can make faces at that dog; that scruffy, old thing.
I can even make barking sounds at him and he can't do one, doggone thing about it.
And I can jump up and down and holler like nobody else and make that old dog scared.
Then I can look at that old dog straight in the eye and put fear in his heart.
You ever seen a mangy, scared old dog? There's one!

Ain't nothin' he can do when I stick my tongue way outta my mouth and blow so hard,
Till my saliva gonna make a mist and dampen my own face, jus' 'cause of that there dog.
Yes, then I'll get my big brotha with his big mouth to yell at him and call him 'old dog'.
We ain't scared one bit. We ain't scared of that dog 'cause Mama's holdin' us tight as ever;
And the old dog is on a leash anyway with his owner way over on the other side of the tracks.
That's right!!!

Jennifer P. Lumley

THAT MESS, STRESS

Fatigue from overwork is one cause of stress.
Sleep deprivation will also cause some stress.
Worrying about the bills surely brings on enormous distress.
This thing called stress knows everyone's address.

Stress takes up residence in your head, heart and chest.
It generates torment to the extent that you can't rest.
Most times I try to ignore it lest I lose my zest;
It's really because I cannot handle stress in excess.

Have you ever seen stress in her favorite party dress?
Getting close, causing anguish and putting your life in distress?
She delights in thinking that you are not likely to protest
As she bears down upon you, determined to take away your best.

Heart diseases, indigestion, ulcers and neurological distress
Are all traced directly to the impact of this mess we call stress.
Gastrointestinal, psychological issues, migraines and all the rest,
Keep you running and seeking a cure for this mess you possess.

A "secret chamber" for contemplation is the place you must find,
To relieve you of this stress mess from you spirit, body and mind;
Avail yourself the resources to make changes in your lifestyle;
Stress will depart from you, and transform your frown into a smile.

Breathe deeply and incorporate exercise in your daily regimen;
You won't solve your problems and you should not be ashamed.
Extend your life, take a walk; develop a healthy eating habit.
Get spiritual, reach out to God; take His hand; you can have it.

I must now confess I have had my share of this mess called stress.
Many times, I was blessed after being put to the test
And learned through experiences, that if stress is to be made less.
You'll need to hold God's hand let Him do what He deems best.

THE ROUNDABOUT

Soldier standing
Gun in arms.
Designing spewing
Water falls.
Words etched and placed
On the concrete slab;
Between trees on the block
Are changing lamps
From red to green;
And now to amber.
Water design changes
To a new wonder.
Someone patiently
Designed this.
A fountain!
But nowhere to make
That penny wish.
Dangerous crossing;
Pretty flowers surrounding;
Mad men driving,
Crazy old ladies searching;
Misunderstanding
The roundabout,
No one seems to talk about.
NOPE…not even the children
Appreciate this labyrinth.
When do you yield?
When do you stop?
Where are the cops?
Another accident
Barely avoided
'Cause he didn't stop.
Didn't know he should

Jennifer P. Lumley

Till school children cussed
At the old fool sweatin'
Sitting stunned; not sure
What his next move should be
At the roundabout.
The roundabout that
No one talks about.

THESE TITLES

You're getting to be a habit with me.
You never treat me like you should.
I love you, hate you;
Peel me a grape and shut up the pot.
Neither one of us should be feeling like this
With pen in one hand and handkerchief
In the other.
If you believe in love then
You must be comfortably ensconced
In a place where we don't hurt.
And guess who's coming to dinner?
Mona Lisa!!!

Jennifer P. Lumley

THE WEATHER REPORT

Today there *may* be a serious storm watch over our area. This *may* shift to the right in the next eight hours or so if an east north east wind pushes up and hits this low pressure system to our south.

It *may* be mostly cloudy and overcast for much of the day, if the sun does not come out and we *may* have a shower or two otherwise we will remain dry and cool. We are keeping an eye out for the sun and a bright day soon but in the meantime take your umbrellas and be careful of the windy conditions and precipitation that *may* take place later on this afternoon.

Temperatures *may* remain mild today and *may* be the same for the next couple of days or so, otherwise we *may* expect a coating or an inch of snow mixed with sleet and freezing rain, which is normal for this time of year. This *may* cause slippery road conditions so be careful if it does.

We will keep the radar on the existing conditions and keep you posted with any changes that *may* take place.

TRANG

Bitter is hot
And sweet it's not;
Anguish and pain
Drives you insane
Sour is wild
Never ever mild
Hurt is strong
Heart is longing
Disappointment stings
No wedding bell rings
Misery and torment
Fret and sweat
Suffer and bleed
Torture and greed
Unmet need
Burning sensation
No explanation
And I am still…
ALIVE!!!

Jennifer P. Lumley

UNRUFFLED

You understand so very well,
When maybe I just don't know
What my next reaction is.
You are able to reach deep
Down inside of you
And feel what's on my heart.
Then with a calm, you quiet the rumbling
Of a fear that may erupt.
I close my eyes as you so
Easily comprehend my vision;
And when I lock my doors against the world,
There you are, to share my dreams.
I love you my brother...ERT LEY!!!

VOICES

Voices express such beautiful sentiments,
In sweet whispers and soft tones;
Like ice cream with sprinkles on top
And a crispy, sugary ice-cream cone.

Some voices are squeaky, some high pitched;
Some voices are velvety smooth and deep.
Some voices sound like a rippling brook
Some voices hypnotize you in a long, deep sleep.

Some voices are meant to scare people;
Some to attract people to make a purchase.
Some voices sing such a happy tune;
Other voices will make you confess.

Some voices speak of one's opinion,
With intimidation or a voice of reason.
Some voices command immediate respect;
Many voices plot and plan treason.

Some voices are so warm and fuzzy
And bring beautiful feelings of comfort;
Some voices can be quite informative
Like the sports caster's sports report.

Some voices echo a truly bad attitude
Some voices come on real strong.
Some voices tell a spiritual story;
Other voices say "Something's wrong".

Some voices are clear and articulate
Showing the measures flow and modulation.
This cadence and proper pronunciation
Reflect inflection, enunciation and elocution.

Jennifer P. Lumley

Some voices are dull and monotone;
Some voices go on ad infinitum;
Some voices are like sunshine on a rainy day;
Others go on and on ad nauseam.

When voices come together in a chorus,
They don't have to be singing a song;
They don't have to be filled with ambiguity,
Or be voices filled with circumlocution.

Rather, we have voices that share poetry;
Word locomotion afloat with sensation.
A colorful vehicle to channel joy to souls;
We are royalty with verbal ostentation!

WHAT MAJORITY?

The Majority,
Yes the Majority,
Between Blacks, Latinos and Asians,
There. There is the Majority of which I speak.
But really, what Majority?
Majority in jail, seeking bail;
Taken from the Plantation to the Penitentiary.
A new consciousness comes around;
But a consciousness oppressed with subtlety;
Anytime, every time there is new awakening,
There is a clever, cunning, complex
But precise method employed to extract from this Majority,
Any potential possibility of positive progress,
Growth and advancement.
Not employment, Something different;
Suppression of the mind.
It's what makes you feel good…for now.

This poor Majority occupy more jail space for a pinch
Than those who conduct the actual trade;
Than those who are the greatest drug consumers.
Analyze and study this:
Jamaica does not produce the kind of drugs
That Jamaicans go to jail for
But the country has become the abyss for trans-shipment,
The exchange point
For those tourists, those terrorists of the mind,
Limiting minds to believe in instant gratification,
Rather than excellence in mental preparation.

Assume the position. Don't become that statistic.
Conscious determination
Orderly arranging life choices

Being enlightened, performing above expectations.

I implore you my people, to remember that the alphabet started with the African.

Scattered though we have become, let us not forget that love started with us too.

We can only afford to have good things written and documented about us.

Remember that I told you this day…BE PREPARED!

You too can be a MIND SHAPER and a CHANGE AGENT BECAUSE YOU ARE IN THE MAJORITY!!!

WHEN NEXT I SEE YOU

When next I see you
What should I bring?
The new poem I've written,
Or a happy song to sing?

When next I see you,
What should I carry?
Must I get there before you
And for a while, just tarry?

When next I see you
What should I take?
Should I make a veggie meal,
Some seafood or a steak?

When next I see you
What should I possess?
Will you leave it up to me
To take a guess? A new dress?

When next I see you
What gift should I bear?
Consider no present for me;
I just want you to be there.

Jennifer P. Lumley

WHISPER IN THE DISTANCE

Is my soul not beating down
The doors of your forgetfulness
And moving you to remember
My sweetness?

Has the touch of me lost its warmth?
Can you not see my caramel
Skin and still feel my powerful presence
Sleeping soundly on your
Pillow?

Can you so quickly forget the
Essence of my rose petals
Engulfing your strong desires
And satisfying your passions?
Or does your memory burn holes
In your mind
And starve you from a distance?

Is my head no longer crowned
With royalty recognized?
And your heart so emptied of
Me, that there is a void?

Have you spilled the perfume of our yesterdays so far that
its fragrance can no longer be enjoyed?

Mountains, rivers, wind and footsteps will forever follow you and
whisper my name!

WHY IS HE A CLOWN?

Mommy, why did he choose to be a clown?
This comic performer all around town,
Who prefers to laugh and not to frown?
And gets you feeling up when you're feeling down?

A clown likes to wear big, silly-looking clothes,
Polka dots and plaids and a red shiny nose;
And a big red bow-tie and ruffles everywhere he goes.
He's a clown because his big boots can hide all his toes.

His mismatched wardrobe must be really bizarre;
His baggy overalls and wigs must come from afar.
He has a cute little bunny and a big pet giraffe.
I know why he's a clown. He likes to make me laugh.

I giggle as he topples and trips and rolls on the floor,
Then gets up again and bumps right into the door.
He's really very funny although he does not speak.
Well that's why he's a clown, performing magic tricks.

He walks and he runs and he juggles and he jumps
And he falls on the floor getting more head bumps
I wonder Mommy, does a clown have a bed?
To fit his big boots and belly and all that hair on his head?

Good Night!

WRITING CONSPIRACY

No further will the distance be
Than the tip of my pen to paper,
In words that bring you to me
And where we are much safer.

The paper eagerly seeks out
Yet another drop of ink on its lines
To keep it quiet company or to shout
Gently settling the echo of each rhyme.

The pen delights in transcribing thoughts
Making action figures of each image,
Conceived and constantly sought,
As mind makes sense of the rummage.

It's as clear as mud but truly, I know,
How pen and paper, in unison, will conspire
To bring love's heart home and never let go;
As my bosom friends they know my desire.

YOHAN BLAKE - 'IM
BELANGS TO JAMAICA

December born, like me;
Nice too, like me;
From St. James, like me
But 'im belangs to Jamaica.

Yuh can imagine di rumpus wah kick up inna Spanish Town
Wen dem hear say Yohan Blake was di one wa cumma around
An win out alla, alla dem an tun di new worl champion!!!

All now some a dem de frown, an bex, an wear lang face
But dat cyaan change di simple fact dat him win di race
An win out, win out alla dem an is di new worl champion!!!

Him hold di national junior record fi di hundred meeta
An bruk di ten second barrier as di youngest sprinter evva
An win out, win out alla dem an is di new worl champion!!!

Him bruk di two hundred meter inna Belgium inna September
An de four by hundred relay we gwine always remember
'Cause 'im win out alla dem an is di new worl champion!!!

And as a part of di Jamacan team, wi bruk wi owna record
Fi Carter, Frater, Bolt an Blake wi haafi say tank God.
Cause Jah is di real, real reason why wi have summuch worl
champions!!!
Dem all belong to Jamaica.

YOU WANT TO MAKE IT HARD

When your well of kindness has overflown and that kindness is taken for granted;
Taken from you as though you weren't going to give it in the first place;
Then spat upon, stepped on, and rubbed in the dirt.
When you make the face of love expansive, inclusive, creative, abundant, and receptive;
And is shoved back at you; no warmth or reciprocity
But total indecent and repeated ingratitude is displayed.

When all the time you put up a front to cover all the stuff; because that's the best thing to call it now;
And that white picket fence is torn down; the house of torment is now the new place of abode.
I see what this is. You want to make it hard; hard for me to love again.
Something good and new must happen.
The sun still shines behind the dark clouds - it doesn't become a part of them.
Dawn will continually break after the darkest hour – it doesn't join it.

Diamonds must go through those processes so they don't remain rough. Yes diamonds, the derivative of the Greek word 'adamos' meaning 'unconquerable';
A source of fascination; imperishable, precious and HARD.
I thank you for these lessons. I really do. I truly do thank you.

NOW I AM REALLY PREPARED...PREPARED TO LOVE... AGAIN!

Z POETESS

Oh yes, yes, yes.
Here is the Poetess
With the curly, blond tress
And yes, full of zest.
She was the Mistress
Of Ceremony at the fes-tivities
And yes, oh yes
She looked the very best
Elegance and grace
In a strapless, brown dress,
Standing next to Rona Best,
Is Jen Ley, the goddess
Of writing, record keeping,
Wisdom and the rest.
Salute the
African Seshat.
Jenuin Poetess!